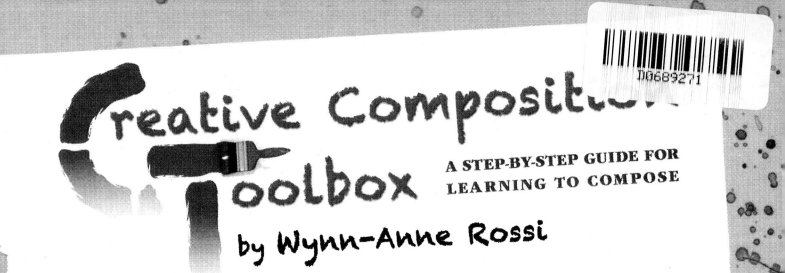

Creative Composition Toolbox

A STEP-BY-STEP GUIDE FOR LEARNING TO COMPOSE

by Wynn-Anne Rossi

Table of Contents

Alfred Music Publishing Co., Inc.
P.O. Box 10003
Van Nuys, CA 91410-0003
alfred.com

ISBN-10: 0-7390-8236-1

ISBN-13: 978-0-7390-8236-2

A Note to Teachers

Creative Composition Toolbox is a practical series that introduces students to the art of original composition. The purpose of this series is to open the world of self-expression to every piano student. The materials can be taught in private lessons, group lessons or as a piano camp. Compatible with any piano method, essential theory skills are reinforced throughout the series in a design that is easy to implement.

Creative Composition Toolbox, Book 1 contains 10 composition tools. Each tool is presented in a two-page format. On the first page, a composition tool is introduced, a sample composition demonstrates the tool, and the student learns by performing it. On the second page, an original composition is assigned that reflects what has been learned.

In *Creative Composition Toolbox,* Book 1, students encounter the following composition tools:

Range	**Damper Pedal**	**Dynamics**	**Tempo**	**Melody**
Harmony	**Repeats and Patterns**	**Conversations**	**Grand Staff**	**Meter**

Students need to write their compositions down so that they do not forget them. Music can be notated in many different ways. *Creative Composition Toolbox,* Book 1 encourages students to use a simple process that can be done using a sheet of notebook paper turned sideways (see example below). Pages 4–19 employ this notation process, allowing the focus of the book to be on *composing* music rather than using strict notation. Also on these pages, the beginning hand position for each piece is shown on a keyboard chart. On page 20, the grand staff is introduced for notating compositions.

❶ *Middle C, represented by a line drawn across the middle of the paper, divides the high and low notes on the piano.*

❷ *Notes are written using the musical alphabet and are placed to approximate the distance from Middle C.*
Fingerings for the RH are above.
Fingerings for the LH are below.

❸ *Notes lined up in the same column are to be played together.*

❹ *A straight horizontal line next to the letter indicates the note value.*

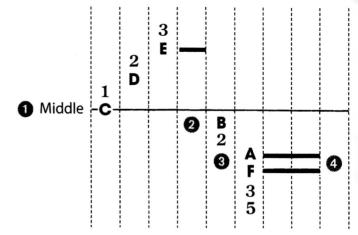

A Note to Students

The piano is an amazing instrument with a very rich history. It has been featured in concerts for kings and emperors throughout the world. Master composers such as Wolfgang Amadeus Mozart and Ludwig van Beethoven have used it to compose famous pieces.

As a beginning composer, you will explore the exciting sounds the piano can make and learn to create your own original music. In *Creative Composition Toolbox,* Book 1, you will learn the tools you need to create compositions in a variety of styles. And, you'll be able to notate your pieces right from the start! Each new composition tool is followed by a piece that features this tool. Then, you will create a piece on your own using the given idea. The **Toobox Tip** sections review important concepts, and the **Composer Connection** presents interesting facts about well-known composers.

So, grab a pencil and turn the page. The exciting world of composition is at your fingertips!

Composition Tool: RANGE

The piano can make both very low and very high sounds. These notes—from lowest to highest—are called the *range* of the piano. They are great for expressing different ideas and feelings. As a composer, it is exciting to explore the full range of the piano.

Lots of music is about animals! Animals are very expressive and have so many different personalities. Imagine a kangaroo hopping up and down the keys. Where is it going? What is it doing?

Kangaroo Romp

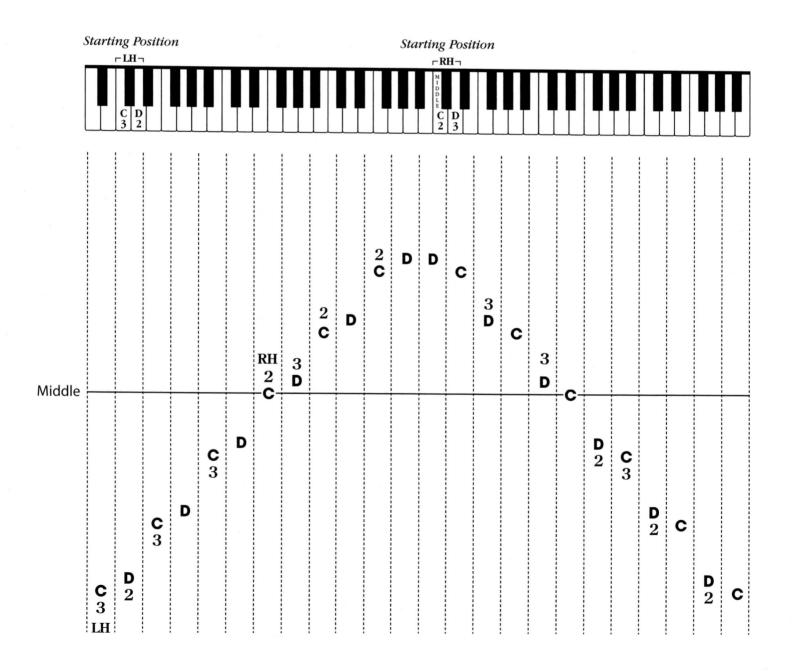

Create Your Own Piece

Spider monkeys swing from tree to tree in the tropical rain forests of South America. Compose a piece about this endangered species using the full range of the piano. What kind of personality does your monkey have? Is it gentle or wild and crazy? If you run out of room while composing, you can use an extra sheet of notebook paper. Turn it sideways and draw a line for Middle C across the paper.

Composer Connection

Johann Sebastian Bach (1685-1750) did not have a piano when he wrote his keyboard music. He used a harpsichord which has a smaller range than the piano. Bach could not compose pieces with very low or very high notes for the harpsichord, but you can for the piano!

Spider Monkey

Starting Position

Composition Tool: DAMPER PEDAL

The pedal on the right is called the *damper pedal* and is a very handy tool for a composer. It makes the sound of the piano "ring" by lifting the dampers off the strings. It can completely change the sound of a composition.

Many composers use nature as an inspiration. Nature can be beautiful but also powerful and exciting. The pedal can help create the sounds of peaceful rain or booming thunder. Try this piece without the pedal. Which way do you prefer?

Thunder and Lightning

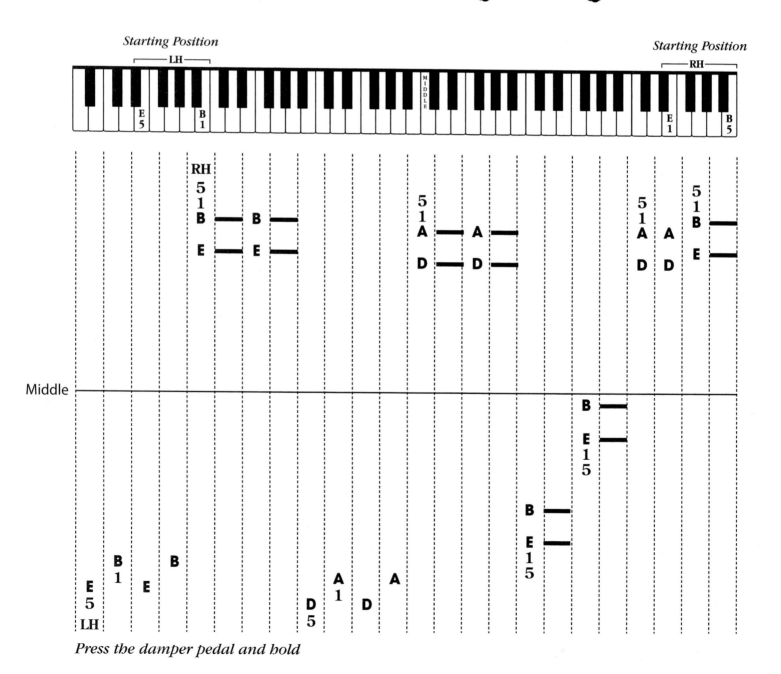

Press the damper pedal and hold

Create Your Own Piece

Compose your own thunderstorm using the damper pedal. How long will it rain? What will your thunder sound like? Is there lightning in the sky? Use your imagination to create a powerful storm!

Toolbox Tip

Using the full **RANGE** of the piano can help you express different ideas and feelings.

Composer Connection

Claude Debussy (1862-1918) loved the damper pedal! He wrote special notes to himself about it. Sometimes he suggested putting the pedal down before beginning a piece so the strings could ring as much as possible.

Lightning and Thunder

Starting Position

Press the damper pedal and hold

Composition Tool: DYNAMICS

Soft and loud sounds in music are called *dynamics*. Dynamics are most often indicated by Italian words that are abbreviated with letters:

$\boldsymbol{p}$ *(piano)* = soft $\boldsymbol{f}$ *(forte)* = loud

What would music be without dynamics? Composers use soft and loud sounds to tell stories and create moods. What is the story in this piece? What is creeping at the bottom of the keyboard in the beginning? What do you think happens next?

Something in My Basement!

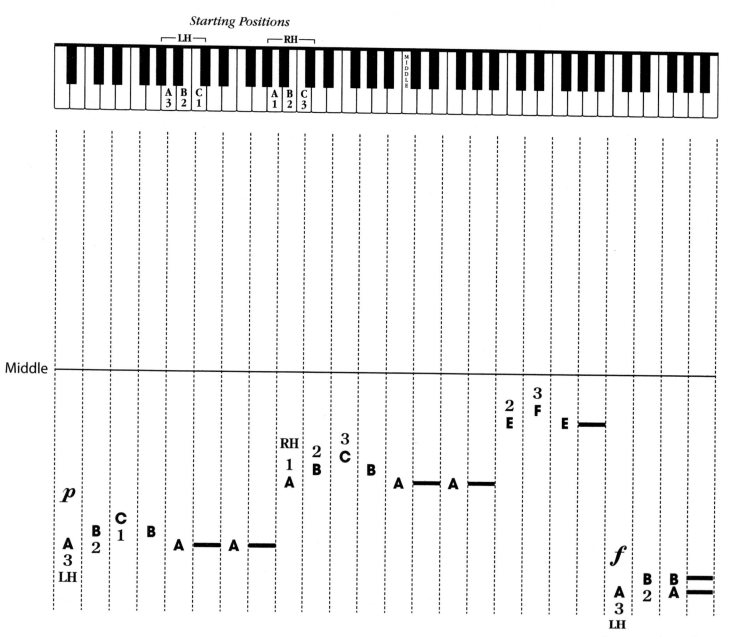

lowest piano key

Create Your Own Piece

Create mystery with soft and loud sounds as you compose this piece about an attic. How do you want people to feel when they listen to it? What is your story?

1. Add your own dynamics.   2. Add the damper pedal.

Toolbox Tip

The **DAMPER PEDAL** makes the notes ring by lifting the dampers off the strings.

Composer Connection

Frédéric Chopin (1810-1849) had a great sense of humor. He enjoyed putting people to sleep with his beautiful, soft playing then waking them up with a loud bang!

Something in My Attic!

Composition Tool: TEMPO

Music sounds very different depending on how fast you play it. The speed at which the piece is played, called *tempo*, is marked at the beginning of every piece. This is very important so performers understand your music.

Do you like playing slow or fast? It is fun being a composer, because you get to decide the speed of your music. In the following piece about a track meet, choose a title then choose a matching tempo.

1. Circle a title.   2. Circle a tempo.

Warming Up, Easy Course, Race for the Finish

Tempo? **Slow**   **Moderate**   **Fast**

Starting Positions

Press the damper pedal and hold

Create Your Own Piece

Compose a piece about a school day. How does your day normally begin? Do you drag your feet, or are you always on the run? Decide which speed fits you. Think about the title and what is going on as you decide which notes to use. Experiment!

1. Circle a title.   2. Circle a tempo.   3. Add dynamics.

Toolbox Tip

DYNAMICS indicate soft and loud and are included in every piece.

Composer Connection

Franz Liszt (1811-1886) composed and performed a lot of music that was really fast and difficult to play. He dazzled people, like a piano rock star. His compositions are so complicated, many pianists cannot play them.

Morning Blues, On the Bus, I'm Late!

Tempo? **Slow** **Moderate** **Fast**

Starting Positions

Composition Tool: MELODY

A *melody* is a line of single notes that forms a musical idea. Many melodies start and end on the same note. They are mostly made with steps and skips. On the piano, a step moves up or down from one white key to the next. A skip moves up or down, skipping over a white key.

A melody line moves up and down like a mountain range. Composing a melody is like creating your own nature path. You take steps and sometimes skip over rocks. Ending on the same note is like coming home after having an exciting adventure. Enjoy hiking on Lookout Mountain!

Lookout Mountain

Tempo: Moderate

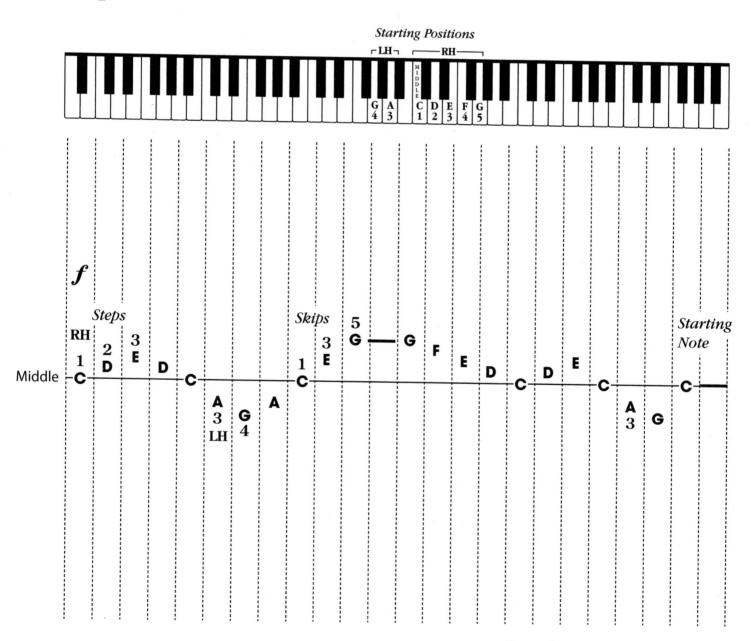

Press the damper pedal and hold

Create Your Own Piece

Create your own mountain melody made of steps and skips. Make a beautiful shape with the notes that you choose. Come home after your journey by ending on the starting note.

      1. Create a title.   2. Choose a tempo.   3. Add dynamics.

Toolbox Tip

TEMPO is the speed at which the piece is played and is marked at the beginning of every piece.

Composer Connection

Edvard Grieg (1843-1907) composed a famous piece for orchestra called In the Hall of the Mountain King. *He used many musical steps and skips to tell the story about a young boy named Peer Gynt. In his story, the mountain king is a troll!*

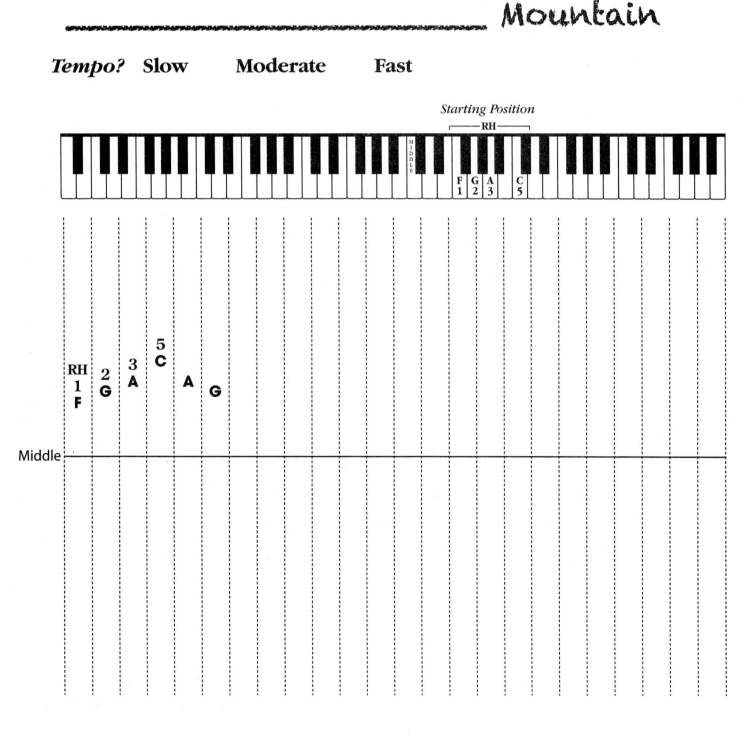

Composition Tool: HARMONY

Harmony is when two or more notes are played at the same time. These extra notes can completely change the feeling of the melody. Certain harmonies feel content and peaceful. Others feel sad, mysterious or even angry.

When you think of harmony, think of the movies! Star Wars *was so much more exciting with music that featured clashing harmonies during fight scenes with Darth Vader. In* The Wizard of Oz, *the munchkins sang music with cheerful harmonies to welcome Dorothy to the magical Land of Oz.*

Movie Magic I

Tempo: Fast

Starting Positions

LH: D5 E4 F3 G2 A1 — RH: D1 E2 F3 G4 A5 (MIDDLE)

Create Your Own Piece

Create a piece with harmonies that would go in your movie! Think about what kind of scene you want. Is it beautiful and peaceful, or is it an action scene? Experiment as you choose your harmonies. They will affect the mood.

1. Choose a tempo.   2. Add dynamics.

Toolbox Tip

A **MELODY** is a line of single notes that forms a musical idea.

Composer Connection

Harold Arlen (1905-1986) composed the song "Over the Rainbow" for the movie The Wizard of Oz. *The editors almost took it out of the movie! They said the movie was too long and thought the song was not important. "Over the Rainbow" has since become one of the most popular songs of all time.*

Movie Magic II

Tempo? **Slow**   **Moderate**   **Fast**

Composition Tool: REPEATS AND PATTERNS

Too many musical ideas can make music sound confusing. Composers repeat ideas to help tie the music together. They also use patterns. A *pattern* is a group of notes that is used in the piece and then used again, beginning on a different note. Rhythm patterns can be repeated, too.

Listening to music without repeats and patterns is like playing a game (such as Simon Says) with someone who does not know the rules. It's very confusing, and nobody enjoys it. However, that does not mean music cannot have surprises… just like the game!

Simon Says

Tempo: Fast

lowest G

Create Your Own Piece

Simon Says, "Compose a piece full of repeats and patterns." Create a game as you play with your musical ideas. Will there be a surprise at the end? Writing music can be fun!

1. Create a title.   2. Choose a tempo.   3. Add dynamics.

Toolbox Tip

HARMONY is when two or more notes are played at the same time.

Composer Connection

George Bizet (1838-1875) composed a set of 12 pieces for piano duet called Children's Games. *Titles in this suite include "Leap Frog" and "Blind Man's Bluff." One old game that Bizet also added was called "Battledore and Shuttlecock" and is similar to the modern game of badminton.*

_____ **Says**

Tempo? **Slow**   **Moderate**   **Fast**

Starting Position ⌐—LH—⌐   *Starting Position* ⌐—RH—⌐

G5 B4 D1   G1 B3 D5

RH 1 G   3 B   5 D

Middle ——————————————————————

D 1

B 3

G 5

LH

p

Composition Tool: CONVERSATION

Music can speak! Notes can "talk" back and forth to each other, similar to a *conversation*. Music with words can make this work even better. Composers sometimes write the words first and then put them to the music.

How do you talk? Sentences and paragraphs. Questions and answers. Loud bellows and soft mumbles. Composers use all of these things in their music, and you can, too.

The Lion and the Eagle

Tempo: Moderate

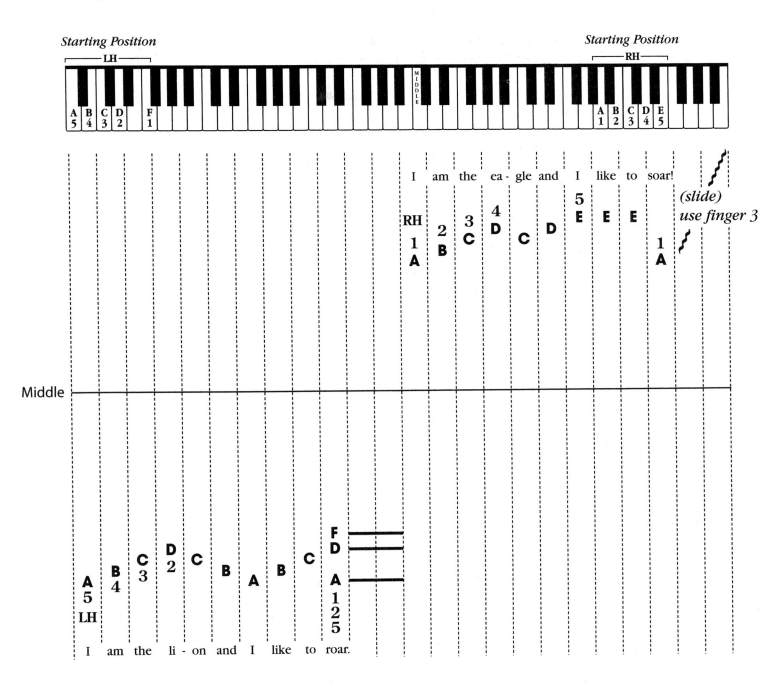

Create Your Own Piece

You can create your own musical composition. Choose two people or animals, then think of interesting words they might say to each other. Put the words to music for your special song.

    1. Create a title.   2. Choose a tempo.   3. Add dynamics.

Toolbox Tip

REPEATS AND PATTERNS help tie music together.

Composer Connection

Camille Saint-Saëns (1835-1921) wrote Carnival of the Animals, *a fantastic suite for two pianos and orchestra. The music depicts an elephant, a swan, kangaroos, tortoises and other creatures. The opening is titled "March of the Royal Lions." The lions roar several times!*

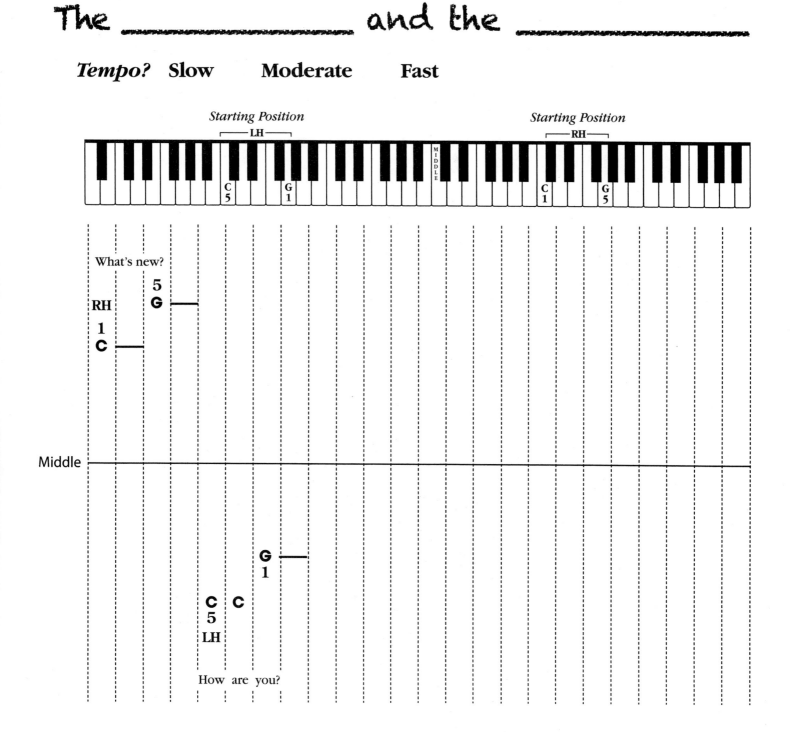

The _____ and the _____

Tempo? **Slow**   **Moderate**   **Fast**

Composition Tool: GRAND STAFF

Welcome to the *grand staff,* a universal form of notation for piano that is used all over the world. Even though people speak many different languages, they can always share music. The grand staff helps make this possible.

Each key on the piano is represented by a note on the grand staff. Middle C is the dividing line between the upper and lower staff. The upper staff is for the right hand, written in the treble clef; the lower staff is for the left hand, written in the bass clef.

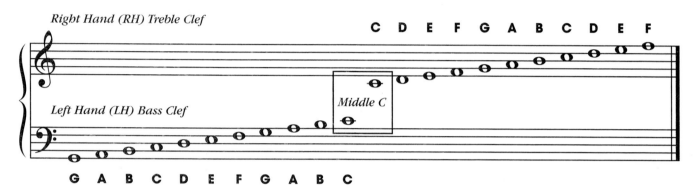

Notice that the grand staff below is divided into boxes by vertical lines, called *bar lines.* Bar lines divide music into *measures.* Each measure must have the same number of beats.

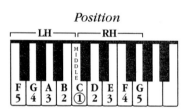

Middle C Madness

Tempo: Moderate

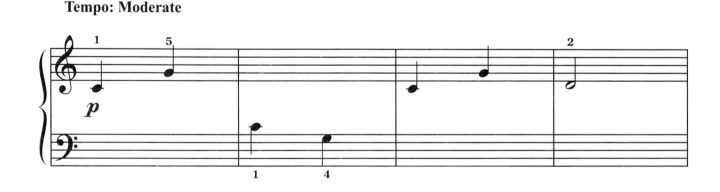

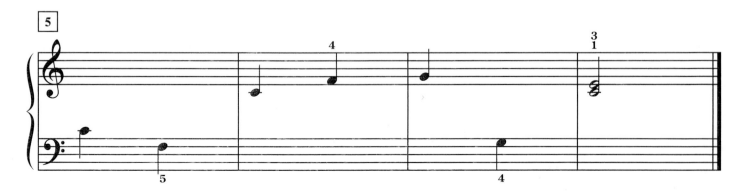

Create Your Own Piece

Compose your own Middle C piece using the grand staff. Each measure has two beats.

    1. Create a title.   2. Choose a tempo.   3. Add dynamics

Toolbox Tip

Notes can "talk" back and forth to each other, similar to a **CONVERSATION**.

Composer Connection

The staff used today came from the 12th century when Gregorian Chants were first notated. Legend honors Pope Gregory the Great (c. 540-604) as the first composer of these chants, but scholars believe they were a combination of European chanting traditions.

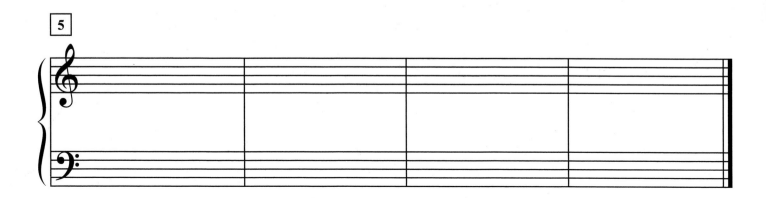

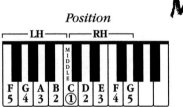

Position

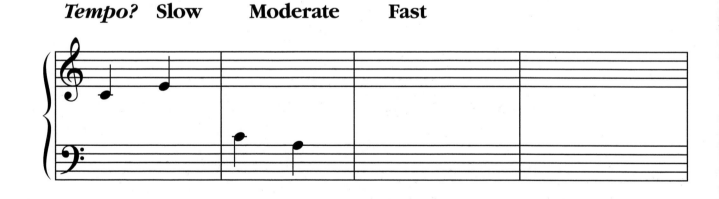

Tempo? **Slow**   **Moderate**   **Fast**

Composition Tool: METER

Music has a regular pattern of beats called *meter*. Meter is shown at the beginning of every piece by the time signature. Meter influences rhythm and affects the sound of music:

$\frac{2}{4}$ = 2 beats per measure $\frac{3}{4}$ = 3 beats per measure $\frac{4}{4}$ = 4 beats per measure

The correct number of beats must be placed into both clefs in every measure. This can be done with either notes or rests. Rests are symbols of silence that mean to lift your fingers from the keys. Rhythm can combine both notes and rests.

♩ or 𝄽 = 1 beat, 𝅗𝅥 or ▬ = 2 beats, 𝅗𝅥. = 3 beats, 𝅝 or ▬ = 4 beats or a complete measure

Imagine motion made into sound! Composers can make this happen. Music can express a rolling ball, a flying plane, a soccer game or even yo-yo tricks!

Yo-Yo Tricks

Tempo: Moderate

Trick #1: "Walk the Dog"

Trick #2: "Ferris Wheel"

Trick #3: "Around the World"

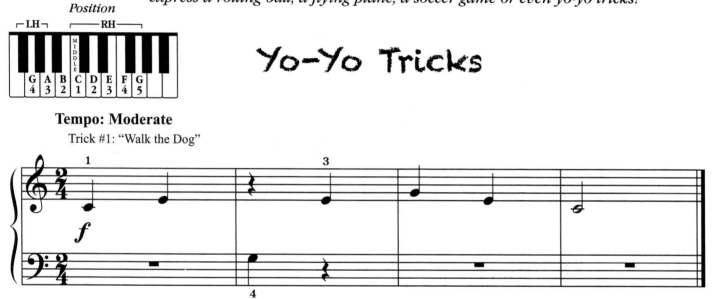

Create Your Own Piece

Compose your own musical juggling tricks! Follow the meters as marked. Place the correct number of beats in each measure for both clefs. Notice how each trick feels a little different because the meters are different. Get creative! One trick may be a warm-up. Another might be faster, with more balls. You can even juggle torches! Give names to your tricks and write them in the blanks.

1. Create titles for you "tricks."   2. Choose a tempo.   3. Add dyanmics.

Toolbox Tip

The **GRAND STAFF** is a universal form of notation for piano.

Composer Connection

Composers can be jugglers of a different kind. In addition to composing, they often perform, conduct and teach. Jerry Goldsmith (1929-2004) juggled a career of composing for both television and movies. He wrote music for five Star Trek films!

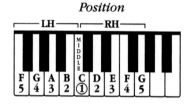

Juggling Tricks

Tempo? **Slow**   **Moderate**   **Fast**

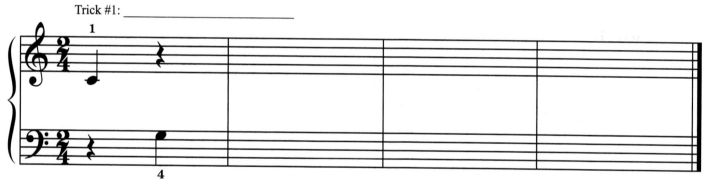

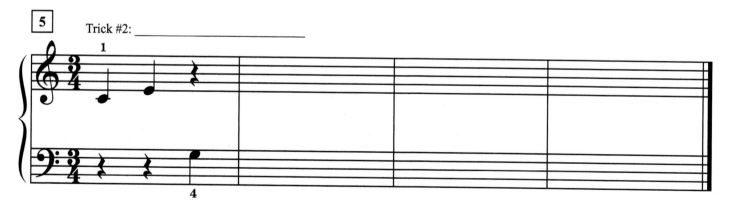

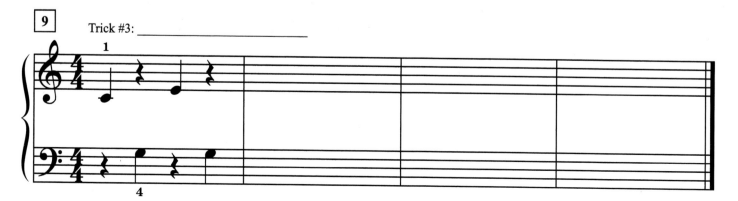

Compose Your Own: OPUS 1

An opus is an original musical work by a composer. Now it is your turn to compose your first opus using the skills you have learned in this book. Look back through the pages for ideas. What kind of mood do you want? Will it tell a story? Do you want words? It is all up to you!

1. Create a title.
2. Choose a tempo.
3. Choose a meter ($\frac{2}{4}$, $\frac{3}{4}$ or $\frac{4}{4}$).
4. Add dyanmics.

Toolbox Tips

- Using the full **RANGE** of the piano can help express different ideas and feelings.
- The **DAMPER PEDAL** makes the notes ring by lifting the dampers off the strings.
- **DYNAMICS** indicate soft and loud and are included in every piece.
- **TEMPO** is the speed of the piece and is marked at the beginning of every piece.
- A **MELODY** is a line of single notes that forms a musical idea.
- **HARMONY** is when two or more notes are played at the same time.
- **REPEATS AND PATTERNS** tie music together.
- Notes can "talk" back and forth to each other, similar to a **CONVERSATION**.
- The **GRAND STAFF** is a universal form of notation for piano.
- **METER** is shown at the beginning of every piece by the time signature.

(Title)

(Tempo)

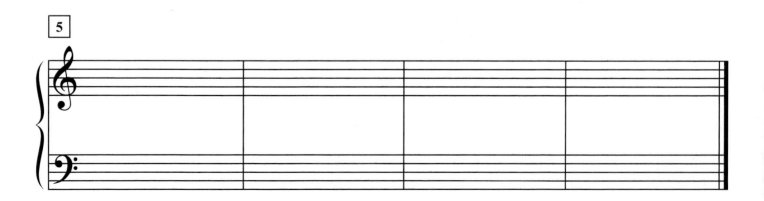